Walter Dean Myers

The Library of Author Biographies™

WALTER DEAN MYERS

Karen Burshtein

The Rosen Publishing Group, Inc., New York

For J. and S. L. and S. and J. G.

Published in 2004 by The Rosen Publishing Group, Inc.
29 East 21st Street, New York, NY 10010

First Edition

Library of Congress Cataloging-in-Publication Data

Burshtein, Karen.
Walter Dean Myers / Karen Burshtein.— 1st ed.
    p. cm. — (Library of author biographies)
Summary: Discusses the life and work of the well-known author of award-winning young adult literature who grew up in Harlem as a foster child and struggled with his identity as an African American writer. Includes bibliographical references and index.
ISBN 0-8239-4020-9 (lib. bdg.)
1. Myers, Walter Dean, 1937– . 2. Authors, American—20th century—Biography. 3. African American authors—Biography. 4. Young adult literature—Authorship. [1. Myers, Walter Dean, 1937– . 2. Authors, American. 3. African Americans— Biography. 4. Authorship.] I. Title. II. Series.
PS3563.Y48Z59 2003
813'.54—dc21

                                                    2003000635

Manufactured in the United States of America

Excerpt from *Something About the Author*, Volume 2, by Adele Sarkissian, Gale Group © 1993, Gale Group. Reprinted by permission of the Gale Group.
Excerpt from *Something About the Author*, Volume 71, by Gale Group © 1993, Gale Group. Reprinted by permission of the Gale Group.
Interview with Walter Dean Myers reprinted by permission of Miriam Altshuler Literary Agency, on behalf of Walter Dean Myers. Copyright © 2003, by Walter Dean Myers.

Table of Contents

Introduction:
Keeping It Real

"**I**s this book autobiographical?" This is a question that is asked often of any novel written by Walter Dean Myers, even when the main character is a teenage girl or a nineteenth-century cowboy. That is because Myers, who has written more than seventy books, mostly about young African Americans, has a real talent for converting nearly every incident that has touched his own life—big or small, good or bad—to material for his fiction. Any ordinary experience that happened to him, especially in his young adult years growing up in New

York City's Harlem, might be the seed of an idea that grows in Myers's imagination into the theme of a whole novel.

For example, after Myers learned that in New York City, abandoned buildings were sometimes sold for almost as little as twenty-five dollars, he spun this information into his novel *The Young Landlords* (1979). The book is about a group of devoted twelve-year-old friends from Harlem who buy a rundown building for a dollar and take on the responsibilities of landlords. Another time, when he was about fourteen, Myers was sitting atop a tree in a park in Harlem, writing poetry when members of a gang surrounded him. He flashed a knife, caught the gang members off guard, jumped from the tree, and ran away. The dilemma of a boy having to chose between being an artist or a member of a gang is one of the underlying themes of his multi-award-winning book *Scorpions* (1988).

Sometimes Myers really stretches a real-life incident. The setting for *The Righteous Revenge of Artemis Bonner* (1994) is the Wild West of the 1880s; the premise for the story is a fifteen-year-old boy from New York who heads west to avenge his uncle's murder. Myers's own uncle was murdered in New York City in the 1940s.

Although he never fought in the Vietnam War, his book *Fallen Angels* (1989), about a kid who leaves his family and home in Harlem to fight in that war, was based on Myers's own experience in the army.

Besides their basis in his real life, Myers's books have other things in common: Most are coming-of-age stories aimed at young adults. This is an important age for Myers because, as he says, "the young adult and middle grade periods of my life were so vivid and, in looking back, so influential in how I would live the rest of my life, that I am drawn to [them] over and over again."[1]

At the heart of Walter Dean Myers's books are the questions and twin feelings of despair and hope that were part of his young adult years. In his books he also writes about the African American experience, courage and survival, complicated family relationships, and facing the consequences of one's actions—all issues he repeatedly faced in his own often-troubled youth.

And yet despite these heavy issues, Myers's books appeal to readers because he never moralizes. Instead, he puts his characters on stage and lets them speak. The backdrop for that stage is often Harlem, the mostly African American neighborhood in New York where Myers grew up. You could even say that Harlem itself is a character in Myers's works; he explores the neighborhood's many dimensions just as he does with his characters. Myers's Harlem is a place both of knife-carrying gangs and of people from a close-knit community lending each other a hand to help get through the day. It is a neighborhood of beautiful parks to read in and rundown tenement building roofs to dream from.

The tell-it-like-it-is style of writing that is Myers's trademark has helped win him many fans and numerous awards; he has collected more than thirty literary prizes for his fiction and non-fiction books, poems, and essays. Among the honors he has received are the prestigious Newbery Honor Award for *Somewhere in the Darkness* (1992) and *Scorpions* (1988). He has won the Coretta Scott King Award—named in honor of the civil rights leader and widow of Martin Luther King Jr.—for his fiction and nonfiction works *Now Is Your Time! The African-American Struggle for Freedom* (1991); *Scorpions*; *Motown and Didi: A Love Story* (1987); and *The Young Landlords*. He has also been given the Margaret A. Edwards Award for his contribution to young adult literature. In 2000, he won the first-ever Michael L. Printz Award (named after a book-loving school librarian) for his novel *Monster* (2000).

Some critics have faulted Myers for making too much of a connection between African Americans and the inner urban experience— after all, not all African Americans live in big cities or tough neighborhoods like Harlem, they say. But this is what Myers knows, and he is a firm believer in the school of thought that says write about what you know best.

Another major lesson for readers of Walter Dean Myers's books is the importance of paying attention to every part of your surroundings. Myers's sharp eye for detail can even make a description of a back alley seem like a magical land. "The tarred streets, the fire escapes upon which we sought relief from the heat, two sewer stickball . . . this was the stuff of dreams"[2] is a typical description of his childhood neighborhood. And his ear for dialogue is as keen as his eye. His books are full of the very real, everyday language of Harlem. *Fast Sam, Cool Clyde, and Stuff* (1975), for example, is written in very authentic black English, and every chapter of *The Mouse Rap* (1990) commences with a rap verse:

> You can call me Mouse, 'cause that's my tag
> I'm into it all, everything's my bag
> You know I can run, you know I can hoop
> I can do it alone, or in a group
> My ace is Styx, he'll always do
> Add Bev and Sheri, and you got my crew
> My tag is Mouse, and it'll never fail
> And just like a mouse I got me a tale.[3]

Several of his books, including *Fallen Angels* (1988) and *Hoops* (1981), have been challenged by school boards and school libraries because of their use of swear words or strong language. Myers defends himself by saying that he is being realistic—this is how his characters would talk, and for him, it's important to remain true to his characters. This also means refusing to tone down the dangerous realities of his characters' rough-and-tumble urban lives. For example, Jamal Hicks, the main character in *Scorpions*, has to choose between joining a gang, as his older brother wants him to, or pursuing his talent as an artist. Will Jamal be able to figure all this out? In *Hoops*, seventeen-year-old Lonnie Jackson's skill at basketball might help "get him over"[4]—in other words, out of Harlem. But Lonnie soon realizes that there is a lot more to life than negotiating your way around the basketball court. He has to learn how to skillfully maneuver his way around the sometimes brutal arena of the Harlem streets. When his coach, Cal, tells him, "You got to learn to use your talent . . . and you got to cover yourself,"[5] Lonnie has to learn for himself what that means.

But even when he tackles difficult subjects, such as homelessness or drug abuse as in *Motown and Didi: A Love Story*, Myers's books have an upbeat mood. The underlying positive message in all his books is that you can succeed if you really try. This was a message Myers himself took a long time to understand. For much of his life, he went through debilitating identity crises and feelings of hopelessness. Even after he started writing, one of his greatest struggles was—and, he will say, continues to be—with his identity as an African American writer. When he was growing up, he wasn't exposed to black American writers with whom he could identify. None were taught in any of the schools Myers attended. Could you be black and a writer? Was being a writer even a real job? Could you like poetry and still be a man?

In time, Walter Dean Myers has come to believe that his books can fill the void in the lives of young African Americans for positive reading experiences and role models. But before he came to this realization, there were many years of wandering. And wondering.

1 The Wonderful World of Harlem

In an article on Walter Dean Myers, a journalist once wrote: "I shall not even attempt to retrace the family tree."[1] Walter's family situation wasn't that confusing when he was born in Martinsburg, West Virginia, on August 12, 1937, but it quickly became jumbled. Walter Milton Myers was the fourth child born to George Myers and Mary Green Myers. His older siblings were Gertrude, Ethel, and George. A baby sister, Imogene, was born shortly after Walter. Walter's father had been married before, to a woman named Florence, and they had two daughters, Geraldine and Viola, who lived with their father. Just after Imogene was born, tragedy struck the Myerses' household: Mary Myers died. George then had seven children to raise alone.

When Mary Myers died, Florence, George's first wife, was remarried to a man named Herbert Dean. She had met Herbert in Baltimore, Maryland, where he grew up. Although Florence and Herbert Dean were happy together, life in Baltimore was difficult for them for several reasons. Florence Dean was half-German, half–Native American, and mixed marriages were frowned upon in the southern United States. They decided to move to New York, where interracial marriages were more socially acceptable. The Deans moved to Harlem, and Herbert Dean got a job as a shipping clerk and janitor at the United States Radium Corporation. The Deans were happy in New York, but Florence Dean missed her daughters, Geraldine and Viola. After Mary Myers died, the families decided that Florence would take custody of the two girls. Shortly after she brought Geraldine and Viola to Harlem, the Deans and George Myers decided that Walter, who was three years old, would go live with the Deans, too.

Right at Home

Walter says he remembers the Greyhound bus ride from West Virginia to New York, and that after moving in with the Deans, he would no longer know hunger. He easily accepted Florence Dean as his "Mama," the name he called her right from the start, even though he called Mr. Dean "Herbert" and not "Dad." (Walter was still known as Walter Myers; he added "Dean" many years later as a tribute to his foster parents.)

Florence Dean was not only "Mama" for Walter, but the greatest mother on earth. Though he says he had no memory of his birth mother, her death must have had an impact on his psyche and easily explains why he clung so strongly to Florence Dean. From the start, he followed Mama around from room to room as she cleaned and scrubbed their small, sunny fifth-floor walk-up apartment on 121st Street.

Three-year-old Walter loved Harlem. He later called it "an exotic land with an inexhaustible supply of delights."[2] Harlem isn't hard to find on a map of New York City. It's a huge section of Manhattan, bounded on the south by Central Park, on the north by the Bronx, on the west by the Hudson River, and on the east by the East

River. In the Harlem of that era, Myers would later write in his autobiography *Bad Boy* (2000), "There were radios everywhere and little girls jumped double Dutch to Duke Ellington, Cab Calloway and Glenn Miller."[3] Myers noted that Harlem legends such as the champion boxer Sugar Ray Robinson were real people he often saw on the street. In fact, Sugar Ray sometimes boxed with Walter and his friends.

Even as a small boy, Walter paid careful attention to sights and sounds. "I remember the bright sun on Harlem streets, the easy rhythms of black and brown bodies, the sounds of children streaming in and out of red brick tenements . . . I remember playing basketball in Morningside Park until it was too dark to see the basket and then climbing over the fence to go home,"[4] he later reminisced.

One of Walter's first memories was of walking to Sunday school on 126th Street. He remembers that a woman took him and "five, sometimes ten"[5] neighborhood children with her to the Bible school. They would walk together holding hands and singing Bible songs on their way to church. Walter came to love Bible school so much that when Florence Dean needed to threaten him with punishment—which would happen a lot—she would warn him that he wouldn't be allowed to attend Bible school.

In those days, before television, children played in the street, and mothers would lean out of their windows to watch them. In fact, the women had special pillows to rest their elbows on while they "street-watched." Much later, Walter would remember the kids he played two-sewer stickball and Chinese handball with. In fact, all the characters in his first book for young adults, *Fast Sam, Cool Clyde, and Stuff*—Binky, Light Billy, and Carnation Charlie—were based on childhood friends.

Family Life

Despite the warmth of the neighborhood and the love of his foster family, young Walter was a handful. Today we might use a more clinical term such as "hyperactive" to describe his boundless energy, which was compounded by the fact that he was the baby of the family, the only boy, and he was used to getting a lot of attention. His older sisters Viola and Geraldine were already teenagers when they moved to New York. If he didn't get his way, he broke his family's prized possessions. Once he stomped on his sister's new watch because his mother wouldn't give him a nickel.

There were more than a few childhood antics. "I had to whitewash the walls in the back of the church twice; once when the minister caught me throwing orange peels on the sidewalk and once when an assistant minister caught a bunch of us trying to lynch another boy. His offense had been to stare at the sun longer than any of us, go temporarily blind, and thus garner [get] more than his share of attention"[6] he recounted.

While Mr. Dean went to work, his wife mostly stayed at home. Sometimes, when they needed extra money, she did day work, cleaning other people's apartments. When that happened, young Walter was placed in the care of neighbors. Separated from his mama, even for only the day, he lost no time getting into mischief. Once, he went out on the sidewalk and did a dance he'd made up so people would throw him pennies. When he had "earned" enough money, he went to the candy store and bought so many red ice pops that his urine turned red. When his mother came home, he told her he was urinating red. Alarmed, she rushed him to the hospital. She thought he was passing blood. So did the doctor until tests confirmed that it was not blood but too much food coloring from too many ice pops. He did, it seemed, anything he could think of to make his mother think he needed her to stay home and take care of him.

Walter could not stand any time away from the special world he and Mama had created for each other. Mrs. Dean treated Walter almost like an adult. She would engage in adult conversations with the four-year-old, waiting for his answers to her questions as if he were the wisest person on earth. Any child would adore that kind of attention, but having someone listen to him was especially significant for Walter because he had a severe speech impediment.

Not surprisingly, the nurturing care of a mother is a theme that appears frequently in Myers's books. Many of his novels, such as *Scorpions*, *Hoops*, and *The Mouse Rap* feature single-parent households in which the mother is raising the family alone. Even though Mr. Dean was present and involved in the Dean household, Myers often depicts the mother as the center of the family in his books. In *The Mouse Rap*, for example, the main character, Mouse, is worried about what will happen to their home if his father comes back: "Is Moms going to let Mr. D (I'm not calling him Dad) move back in?"[7] Mouse wonders.

One of Walter's most enduring childhood memories was of his mother reading to him from the warmth of their tiny kitchen. Mrs. Dean didn't read much, but she liked romance magazines. She would read sentimental stories from *True Romance* magazine to Walter, and although he couldn't care less about the mushy love stories, as he would later recall, "the sound of mama's voice in our sun-drenched Harlem kitchen was like a special kind of music, meant only for me. It was almost a secret language, one that only the two of us understood."[8] Very soon, sitting side-by-side with his mother, he learned to read.

However, in the Dean household Mama wasn't the only one who told stories. His foster father, Herbert Dean, would take young Walter on his lap and tell wonderful tales about ghosts or frightening creatures. Herbert had a wonderful imagination and a great storytelling voice. The characters in the stories sounded so real that Walter would jump up and run out of the room when they became too scary. Walter's father never read him stories; the tales he told came from his imagination or were passed down in his family.

As Walter would learn when he was much older, Mr. Dean was illiterate, having dropped out of school in the third grade. This truth especially saddened Walter after he had become a successful writer because he very much wanted his father to read his books.

In fact, from the start of his teenage years, Walter would begin to feel that his parents couldn't understand him, and there would come to be much tension in the Dean household. This feeling of mutual incomprehension between parent and child and the fact that the Deans were his second set of parents would, perhaps unconsciously, feed one of the major themes of Walter Dean Myers's novels: the notion of dual families—one to be found at home, and one on the street (in the form of a gang, for example, or a sports team). But for his first years in Harlem, the Deans were unquestionably the center of Walter's secure world.

2 Books, Brawls, and Basketballs

Walter's early years, within the warmth of his storytelling family and the tight-knit Harlem community, might have been peaceful and happy, but school was a totally different story. Walter was bursting with confidence when he entered first grade at P.S. 43 in Harlem. After all, at home he was king of the castle. He was used to having his mother listen to his every word with adoration. But at school no one listened to Walter that way. In fact, every time he opened his mouth, his classmates laughed at him. Walter's severe speaking disability made his speech sound garbled. To his ear, however, the words sounded perfectly fine. When people asked him to repeat himself, he became agitated.

His classmates mocked his speech, and quick-tempered Walter responded angrily. Years later, after he had become a successful writer, he told a group of students, teachers, and parents who had come to hear him speak at a library in Milwaukee, Wisconsin, "If you couldn't understand me, I hit you. I hit boys, I hit girls, I hit teachers."[1] Because of his speech problem, people thought that Walter was not very smart, although this was not the case. His first-grade scores, for example, indicated that he was reading at the second-grade level. But his teachers didn't seem to be able to tell the difference between behavior and intelligence. His third-grade teacher, fed up with the boy's fighting, failed him in all his subjects including reading, at which he excelled.

Over the years, Walter would get to be quite familiar with the principal's office—he was frequently sent there for disciplinary action. (Even then, his eye for detail and his gift for gathering information was apparent. He would later note that he liked being sent to the principal's office because he enjoyed hearing the teachers talk about what they did the night before or what they had for dinner, "just as if they were normal people."[2]) He preferred being sent to the principal's office than to the closet, which was how his third-grade teacher punished him. Despite his tough-guy demeanor, he was terrified of the closet; that was where the monsters lurked in the stories Herbert Dean told him.

A Wonderful Secret

Walter looked for an escape from the cruelty of the real world. He found two: comic books and basketball. He adored reading comics, but then an overly opinionated neighbor, Mrs. Dodson, told his Mama that comics were a bad influence, "a roadmap to the jailhouse,"[3] and Mrs. Dean promptly forbade Walter from reading any more. This naturally made comics even more appealing to the mischievous boy. He would sneak them into the house under his pants legs.

Soon Walter wouldn't have to sneak them in. At the height of World War II, Herbert Dean had been drafted into the U.S. Navy, and Mrs. Dean went to work full-time. During World War II, many of the jobs traditionally done by men were taken over by women. It was the first time in American history that women entered the workforce in significant numbers. Florence

Dean and her daughters, Gertrude and Viola, got jobs in factories in New York's garment district. The house was soon empty when Walter came home, and he could read as many comic books as he wanted in his sunny bedroom. From that point on, books would come to be a secret "vice" for Walter.

Mrs. Conway

Although most of Walter's teachers remained on his case (and he usually gave them reason to), there was one exception: Mrs. Conway, his fifth-grade teacher, who would eventually see the potential in the troublemaker. She would later inspire him when writing the character of Mrs. Brown, the teacher in *Scorpions* who praises Jamal's paintings. However, things didn't start off so well. In fact, as fifth grade started, Walter was pretty sure Mrs. Conway was the nastiest teacher yet. She was constantly punishing Walter, forbidding him to participate in class activities and sending him to the back of the class. The only good thing about fifth grade, Walter decided, was a new boy in his class, Eric Leonhardt. Eric was a white, blond German American boy whose parents owned a bakery in Harlem. Both were bright energetic boys who felt a bit like outsiders. He and Walter became best friends.

One day, after Mrs. Conway asked the class to write a poem, she began to look at Walter differently. As usual, she had sent him to the back of the class, and as usual he took out a comic book. Mrs. Conway stomped to the back of the room, snatched the comic from his hand, and tore it to pieces. "You are a bad boy, a very bad boy,"[4] she shouted. (*Bad Boy* would become the title of Myers's autobiography.) But then Mrs. Conway went to her desk, grabbed a book (a collection of Scandinavian fairy tales), and tossed it to Walter. "If you're going to sit back here and read, you might as well read something worthwhile,"[5] she said. "It was the best thing that ever happened to me,"[6] Walter recounted years later. Walter quickly read the book. The next day she brought in more books for Walter. He devoured them all.

Mrs. Conway would help Walter with his speech impediment, too. She had asked each student to read a poem out loud in class, something Walter hated to do. But Mrs. Conway told the class they could read something that they had written themselves. Walter wrote a poem using only words that he was able to pronounce. His classmates were as impressed as the teacher with Walter's poem. Walter's punching days were behind him.

Fighting with Writing

From the moment Walter realized that he could communicate more easily with words he wrote, rather than words he spoke, he became a writer. And like anything else he took to, he did it obsessively, churning out dozens of poems and short stories. One of his first poems was published in the school magazine. It was called "My Mother." Walter also discovered the public library on 125th Street. He couldn't believe there existed a place where you could read books for free, as many as you liked. Walter read everything from *Little House on the Prairie* and *Huckleberry Finn* to works by nineteenth-century poets such as Alfred Tennyson and Elizabeth Barrett Browning, and foreign-adventure writers like Rudyard Kipling. He especially liked stories about faraway places and sunken boats and monsters, like the ones his father told him.

Walter also liked the idea that the librarians thought of him as a serious reader. However, he did not want the kids on the street to think that. He brought books home from the library in a brown paper bag so no one would laugh at him.

His Other Love

No one ever laughed at Walter on the basketball court, where he spent almost as much time as he did at the library. Walter could really "hoop." He was tall; by age eleven he was nearly six feet tall and had learned a good, flat jump shot in the low-ceilinged church basement where he and his friends used to shoot baskets. Walter even played with the well-known basketball player Connie Hawkins, on whom he would later base the main character in *Hoops*, and he once played one-on-one with the legendary Wilt Chamberlain in a Harlem playground.

Like writing, basketball was a way to express himself that didn't require speaking. Walter became so good that some coaches thought he might have a chance to make it in the professional leagues. His parents couldn't have been happier. Athletes were highly respected in their community. And though he loved both books and sports, his twin loves would also be at the root of a growing identity crisis.

Even as a child, Walter refused to blindly accept one-dimensional truths. Just knowing that the community thought of basketball as an accepted path out of the ghetto, for example, made Walter stubbornly refuse to take that obvious route. This refusal to be pigeonholed was a theme that he would repeat in many areas of his life and that would be revisited in many of his books. For example, in *Hoops*, the main character, Lonnie (who gets out of Harlem by being a good ball player), says, "I wasn't going to dance for nobody, and I wasn't going to hoop for nobody."[7]

Though he loved books, they were also a cause of anxiety. Walter wasn't sure how a person could like both sports and books. Years later, Walter would say that, at that time, there were "two very distinct voices"[8] in his head: "One had to do with sports, street life and establishing myself as a male. It was a fairly rough voice, the kind of in-your-face tone that said I wouldn't stand for too much nonsense on the basketball court or in the streets."[9] But every time that voice "spoke" inside his head, another would ask it: What kind of sports-loving male likes poetry? The way he saw it, either he was a sellout to his culture and community or he was giving in to ideals the community had carved in stone and was selling out to himself. It wasn't until many years later that Myers would come to the conclusion that "it is acceptable to be an African American from the inner city, a basketball player, and a voracious [insatiable] reader." But at the time, young Walter was sure these "different" identities were "mutually exclusive."[10]

The Identity Crisis Continues

Around the age of twelve, just as he was beginning to ask himself these questions, a person entered Walter's life who would further his crisis of self. (Years later, however, this crisis would inspire him to write *Somewhere in the Darkness*, his first Newbery Honor Award book, which highlights Walter Dean Myers's ability to turn suffering into a wonderful narrative.) His biological father, George Myers, moved to New York with his new wife and family. Walter would later say that, at the time, he didn't make much of George Myers's arrival. For him, this man was just George Myers, and Herbert Dean was his father. When George came to greet him, Walter simply shook his hand.

And yet something was going on in his subconscious. *Somewhere in the Darkness*'s main themes are the meaning of father-son relationships and the quest for identity. In the book, the main character, Jimmy, lives with his grandmother Mama Jean. One day out of the blue, his father, Crab, comes into his life. Jimmy hasn't seen his father for eight years because Crab has been in prison. Now Crab wants Jimmy to come live with him. Jimmy is faced with the dilemma of leaving the security of his life with Mama Jean to get to know a total stranger who is also his father. In an interview Myers gave when the book was published, he said he didn't know why, but he had to write that book. As he stated, *"Somewhere in the Darkness* is one of those books that come out of the dark areas of the writer's mind."[11]

3 Dead White Poets and . . . Me?

L ike Mrs. Conway, Walter's sixth-grade teacher, Irving Lasher, was someone who came to understand the potential lurking inside the "bad boy." And there still was quite a bit of bad boy to Walter. For example, on the third day of sixth grade, Walter kicked Mr. Lasher in the butt. Mr. Lasher went to see Florence Dean, but instead of mentioning the kicking incident, he surprised Walter by telling Mrs. Dean that Walter was a gifted child with superior reading and testing skills and that something should be done to help him realize his potential. We need more bright black boys, not more tough black boys, Mr. Lasher had told Mama.

34

"He gave me permission to be a bright kid, permission to be smart,"[1] Myers recalled. Mr. Lasher gave Walter leadership roles in class and sent him to speech therapy one day a week. Thanks to Mr. Lasher, Walter graduated sixth grade at the top of his class and even got an award for outstanding work.

Walter took an admission test for Stuyvesant High School, a school for New York City's brightest students. He was admitted, and remarkably, his best friend Eric was, too. Despite the honor of being considered one of the brightest kids in New York, Walter's four years at Stuyvesant would be a "disaster," as he would later say. He would spend them dropping out and dropping back in, then finally dropping out for good, just before his class graduated.

The reasons for this were complex. It was more than his disappointment at learning that Stuyvesant was an all-boys school and more than having to take the subway for longer than an hour each way to get there and back. By the time he started Stuyvesant, Walter was entering a deep depression. His questions about identity had become more pressing, and as he later wrote in *Somewhere in the Darkness* (with reference to the main character, Jimmy), more and more frequently he "was thinking about whether or not he would go to school. He told himself that he didn't feel like it . . . Jimmy had managed the ninth grade fairly well, but the tenth was going badly. He hadn't figured out exactly why. Somehow things were just falling apart. It had happened before but usually he could pull things together."[2]

While he was at Stuyvesant, Walter had to face the difficult reality of racism. Having lived in the mostly segregated Harlem of the 1940s, it was something he hadn't had much experience with. As he later recalled in *Bad Boy*, "For the first time in my life I was faced with the notion that I would have to deal with the idea of race as a central part of my life."[3] At Stuyvesant, Walter's best friend Eric began getting invitations to parties that Walter was excluded from because of his color. Soon their friendship became very, very strained.

Myers would later bring to *Slam!*, published in 1992, the pain and sense of frustration he had felt at people's racist attitudes. In the book, based largely on his Stuyvesant years, Greg "Slam" Harris, a boy from Harlem, transfers to a citywide school for the elite. He is surprised by the insensitivity and ignorance of his teachers and peers. For example, Slam and one of his white classmates are paired up to work on a video. The girl sees Slam's ghetto as having great commercial potential for a film. But, for Slam, it's just his 'hood, a place where real people lead real lives. A teacher agrees with Slam that the girl's attitude is insensitive. But the teacher makes a careless remark himself, provoking Slam almost to rage when he asks him if his use of the word "'be' is directly from [his] African background? Maybe from the We-Be tribe?"[4]

What Is the Point of Being Bright?

Another factor in Walter's depression was that, although he liked learning and he wanted to go to college, he knew that his parents couldn't afford to send him. This angered and confused him. Here he was, an official "bright" kid, and yet college was out of his reach. The reality, as Walter saw it at the time, was that even if you were smart, it was impossible to escape the realities of poverty and racism.

Black colleges such as Spelman and Howard University, existed, and he might have tried for a scholarship at one of them, but for Walter, "black college" implied "voluntary segregation,"[5] and by then he had established, as he called it, his "own avenue of values."[6] In other words, Walter refused to be condemned to one chosen path. He rejected the idea of a "black" college in the same way he rejected the idea of basketball being the only way out of Harlem. As he later put it, he would not allow people to make "a quick and simple decision as to who [he] was."[7] Myers refused to be labeled. He was more than a "black," a "jock," or a "reader."

While Walter's parents thought he was at school, Walter would spend his days wandering around New York. Mostly, he went to Central Park and read philosophical books about the meaning of life by European writers such as Jean-Paul Sartre, Honoré de Balzac, and Friedrich Nietzsche. Sometimes, he would go sit near the Hudson River and write gloomy poems. If he had money, he went to the movies. At night he would lock himself in his room and ask himself the meaning of justice and God and writing and sex. His feelings about girls were the confused feelings of most teenage boys, but rather than exploring the world of dating and possibly facing rejection, he preferred to avoid the issue altogether. In any case, after he discovered books, Walter said he didn't feel much "need to be a social creature."[8]

Black Writers?

Things were kind of falling apart at home, too. Mr. Dean was working to keep the family going at a bare minimum, and Mama was tired of the endless poverty. Then Mr. Dean's brother was murdered in a fight, sending Mr. Dean into a deep depression. Mama could not cope with her husband's state. But rather than sympathize with Mama, Walter began to resent how he felt she used him as an ally against her husband. Conversations with his parents "instead of deepening had become more and more guarded."[9] Then Mama began to drink and gamble.

As always, books were Walter's refuge. But, they, too, troubled him. In all the books he was reading, Walter couldn't find any stories about kids living the kind of experiences he was living or about kids his age in Harlem. He began to fear that even literature would exclude his reality. As the journalist Sarah Brennan would later write on Teenread.com:

> As much as Myers loved reading and was obviously a gifted writer—perhaps the only positive things his teachers ever had to say about him—his interest in these things did not offer him solace [comfort] from the ever-looming angst of adolescence as they would for some teens. Rather, his passion for great works of literature was one of the primary contributors to his ever-deepening identity crisis . . . For Myers the typical existential [philosophical] questions facing a teen—Who am I? What am I going to do with my life? Does anyone really understand me?—were made infinitely more complex by the fact of his race and cultural influences.[10]

Walter couldn't stop asking himself questions: How could the world of words have any place for a street kid like him? Why would a kid, who sometimes carried a knife, even like poetry? In his mind poets were white, eighteenth-century English romantic poets, such as John Keats—"young white men with flowing hair"[11]—or the contemporary Welsh poet Dylan Thomas who wrote moody poems in a language that was often incomprehensible.

The fact is, there were several very talented black writers from Harlem. Authors such as Countee Cullen and Langston Hughes were part of what was known as the Harlem Renaissance of the 1930s, but none were taught at Walter's school. "Books transmitted values. They told us who was important," Myers told an audience in Milwaukee, Wisconsin, many years later. "But the books never mentioned that anyone who lived in my neighborhood was important."[12]

In his memoir *Bad Boy*, Myers remembered running into Langston Hughes on the streets of Harlem. But seeing a famous black writer didn't help Walter's growing conflict about being black and a writer: "Walking with my brother along Seventh Avenue, I once saw a gathering around a brown-skinned man who was being interviewed by some white reporters. Mickey and I went over and found that the man was Langston Hughes. We listened to him talk. He sounded like any black man on the street. There was nothing extraordinary about him . . . I was disappointed. When I pictured the idea of 'writer' in my mind, pictures from my schoolbooks came to mind, and Hughes did not fit that picture."[13]

Harlem no longer seemed like the magical land it had been when he was a child. His negative feelings about the neighborhood extended to his foster parents, too, who, he thought, symbolized Harlem's poverty and ignorance. When Walter was sixteen, he got a part-time job so he could buy a new typewriter. But Mrs. Dean gambled away the money he earned. Mr. Dean bought Walter a used typewriter from a pawnshop—an old-fashioned glass-sided Royal. Walter did not appreciate his father's gesture; the old Royal, Walter thought, underlined Mr. Dean's ignorance. For several weeks, Walter used the typewriter to type only "I hate this typewriter"[14] over and over again, plastering the sheets of paper with that message all over the apartment. Soon though, it became the vehicle for the endless stream of short stories and poems Walter couldn't stop himself from writing. He entered one of the long narrative poems he wrote in a contest and won a set of encyclopedias.

However, this recognition did not help his confidence. He continued to worry about his future. Even if somehow he did get to college, he was sure that racism would prevent him from getting a decent job afterward: "My definition of a black man was, except for the rare exception, a man without an exceptional career, and a man who had to define his maleness by how muscular he was,"[15] he later said.

Walter was convinced he would end up doing manual labor like many members of his family, pushing clothes racks up and down the garment district in New York City or loading trucks. To Walter, the future seemed like a dead end any which way he turned.

4 One Foot over the Edge

Walter's downward spiral continued. Mrs. Liebow, his English teacher at Stuyvesant, who always thought Walter was a gifted writer and had given him lists of books she thought he should read, tried to help him. On one of the rare occasions he bothered to go to school, she told him, "Whatever happens, don't stop writing."[1] Mrs. Liebow would be the name Myers would give Richie Perry's teacher in *Fallen Angels*, and her concern for Walter would resurface in that book when the fictional Mrs. Liebow tells Richie, "You have to get out of yourself . . . You're too young to be just an observer in life."[2] However, despite his teacher's concern, Walter himself was increasingly attracted to "observers," whether they were fictional characters or real people. He was especially interested in a book called *The Stranger* (1942), written by the French author Albert Camus. In *The Stranger*, the main character, Meursault, doesn't have any feelings, as the book's famous opening lines indicate: "Mama died today. Or yesterday maybe, I don't know."[3]

Walter also became friends with Frank Hall, a boy a few years older than himself, who reminded him of Meursault. Frank was a troubled boy: He was homeless, sleeping in hallways and the park, and drinking and dealing drugs. After Walter had dropped out of Stuyvesant, he spent almost all his time with Frank, who would lead Walter on a dangerous path. One night, Walter went with Frank on a drug delivery to a bad neighborhood, where they barely escaped an attack by a gun-wielding gang. That was enough to put an end to Walter's drug-dealing days. Writing of the experience in *Bad Boy*, Myers said: "The gang thing scared me. I didn't mind at all hurting people. That was one thing I had in common with them, and they understood that. But that wasn't the life I wanted to lead. It was no better than being condemned to the garment-center labor force."[4]

Deep down Walter knew he wanted to belong somewhere. But where?

A Break from the Questions

Soon all Walter wanted was a break from the questions constantly swirling around his head. He dreamed of an existence where other people would do the thinking for him, if only for a while. That world would turn out to be the army. The army was about taking orders; it was "an atmosphere of non-thinking,"[5] which appealed to Walter. The emotions he felt then would later influence him when he was writing *Fallen Angels*. The main character, seventeen-year-old Richie, wanted to be a philosopher even though, as he says, "I'm not really sure what a philosopher does."[6]

> I had wanted to win badly. I knew I was going into the army, but for me that was a kind of defeat. My plans, maybe just my dreams really, had been to go to college, and to write like James Baldwin. All the other guys in the neighborhood thought I was going to college. I wasn't, and the army was

the place I was going to get away from all the questions.[7]

Just before his seventeenth birthday, Walter joined the army. He had a romanticized view of war, part of which came from reading the poems of Rupert Brooke, who had fought in World War I. The reality of the army was, of course, much different. Walter did not anticipate how much real combat experience could mess with your head. Of his three years in the army, Myers said that besides spending a good deal of time drinking at the army exchange, "I spent most of my time in the service playing basketball." And he said sarcastically, "I learned several efficient ways of killing human beings."[8]

As it turned out, the army didn't give him a break from all his questions, and because of this, when he later wrote *Fallen Angels*, he would choose to do it in an interesting way: Even though it is a war story, almost all the action goes on in Richie's head. We never see the fighting. Instead we read about Richie's thoughts as he sees the horror going on around him.

Three years after signing up, Myers was discharged. He moved back in with his parents, the Deans, who by now had left Harlem and were living in the suburb of Morristown, New Jersey. The army was supposed to have given him confidence and maybe also answer a few of the questions he had about life. Instead, he found himself back where he started.

5 A Soldier Comes Home to Nowhere

Myers was now convinced that his father's go-nowhere career was destined to be his future as well. He hadn't brought home any real skills from the army; he didn't have a college or even a high school degree. And so, Myers stepped on to his worst nightmare—the manual labor treadmill. For bull work, as his father called it, all you needed was muscle. His worst fears had come true. Here he was working, like most of the people he knew from Harlem, in a factory. A series of low-skill jobs followed the factory job; he worked sorting mail in a Wall Street mailroom, then in a rehabilitation center. He got a job at the post office.

But Myers was fired from the job because he couldn't stand the routine. He was also fired from a job he held for three years, from 1966 to 1969, at the New York State Department of Labor. Then he worked as a messenger.

After a few frustrating years with his parents, Myers moved back to New York City. Shortly after that he met a woman named Joyce and they soon married (they would later divorce in 1970). The couple had two children, Karen and Michael. But not even these happy events could shake Myers out of his sluggish state. Meanwhile, he had all but given up writing. And he was still doing bull work. But his latest job at a construction site would be the last straw. One day, while on the site, a passerby gave Myers a look that he interpreted as pity or disgust. It was too much for him, and he decided once and for all to take charge of his life. That night, Myers bought some notebooks, and every evening he would fill them with new stories.

Being Published

Myers started sending his stories to magazines and newspapers. Most of the time, he got rejection slips, but he didn't even seem to mind that.

For him, the fact that he was writing and sending stories to magazines was a start; it proved that he existed. And soon enough, some of his stories did get published. Within about a year, Myers was writing steadily for many different kinds of magazines: men's magazines, Sunday newspapers, poetry journals. He wrote stories for mystery magazines and even for the *National Enquirer*. He wrote for publications aimed at African American readers, such as the *Liberator*, *Essence*, *Black World*, and *Negro Digest*. He covered sporting events all over the world—bullfighting in Peru, for example, and kickboxing in Japan. Myers knew that the more stories he published, the more his name would be known. And yet when readers actually started recognizing his name, he still wasn't satisfied. He soon realized that it wasn't fame he wanted. Instead, he wanted his writing to reflect the kind of experiences he had growing up in Harlem.

Hopeful and Horrible

Myers started hanging out with writers and artists he met at bars in New York City. One of them, the well-known writer John O. Killens, suggested that Myers enter the Harlem Writers Guild, an association of mostly African American writers. That was the first step for Myers to start seeing writing as more than a hobby or an exercise in validation, but as a real career. And yet, as ever, life was still a mixture of the hopeful and the horrible for Myers. He started spending many late nights in bars with his artist and writer friends, and some of them were drinking heavily and using drugs. This situation caused problems in his relationship with Joyce. Their marriage began to unravel, and eventually, she divorced him.

Although Michael and Karen lived with their mother, Myers remained close to his children. Karen and Michael would also be part of the inspiration for the book that became a major breakthrough in Myers's career. In 1969, Myers entered his children's story, *Where Does the Day Go?* in a contest run by the Council on Interracial Books for Children. The story is about a father who takes his children and their friends to the park. At the end of the day, the children ask him where the day goes. Each child gives his own explanation for why night comes. For example, one child, Karen, thinks the day breaks into little pieces and becomes stars. At the end of the story, the father provides the real reason for why night falls. The story won first prize in the competition.

And, in 1969, at the age of thirty-two, Myers had published his first book.

No More Bull Work

The next year, Myers got a full-time job as an editor at the Bobbs-Merrill Publishing Company. Though he had no experience as an editor, he was offered the job because Bobbs-Merrill felt they needed a black editor. At the time, they didn't have any African Americans on staff. From behind an enormous desk in his own office, Myers undertook his first assignment: editing *Gemini*, a book by the African American poet Nikki Giovanni. Myers learned a lot about what publishers were looking for in a book, which would be helpful to him later when writing his own books.

Aside from the job, there were other reasons to be hopeful about the future. In 1973, Myers married for a second time. Constance Brendel—known as Connie—would help Myers with his alcohol problem and was supportive of his writing. They had a son, Christopher. Myers had a happy marriage; three children, Karen, Michael, and Christopher; and a job at the publishing company.

In 1974, things looked even better. An editor had read a story Myers had written, and though he liked it, he thought it was only the first chapter of a book. Myers had written it as a short story, but because of the editor's interest, on the spot, Myers thought up a continuation of the story and described it to the editor, stretching his short story into a full novel. The editor gave him a contract immediately. That story became *Fast Sam, Cool Clyde, and Stuff*. Published in 1975, it was Myers's first book for young adults. The story is told by Stuff, a nineteen-year-old who is looking back on his youth in Harlem: his friends, their world of broken homes and problems with the police, and the "good people" gang they formed in response to the tension of their inner-city life. The book was a critical and popular success. One reader thought Myers's portrayal of ghetto life in the '70s among young people was "about as accurate as it was funny."[1]

Walter Dean Myers Is Born

Myers received many letters from young adults who admired the natural language in the book. They also enjoyed the book's humor and thought that it was a positive portrayal of inner-city youth. Myers knew he had lots of material like this; his whole youth in Harlem was full of funny and sad stories and characters. All he had to do was turn the material into books. You didn't have to be white and European to be a writer after all!

Fast Sam also marked the first time Myers was published under the name Walter Dean Myers. To honor his foster parents, whom he had come to accept as strong and positive influences in his life, he took their last name as part of his name.

But just as things were finally going his way Myers hit another snag. His bosses at Bobbs-Merrill Publishing Company told him that restructuring in the company would force them to cut some jobs, and they would have to let him go. The idea of looking for another job and possibly having to go back to the hated bull work so soon after his first success as a writer alarmed Myers. But this time around, he decided he was going to be optimistic about the future for a change.

6 The End of the Tunnel

Myers would soon believe that leaving Bobbs-Merrill was the best thing that could happen to him. After all, things weren't so bad. He had signed a contract to write a new book, and that gave him confidence. His fears about having to go back to bull work quickly dried up. He decided he was going to do what he really wanted most: write full-time, even though not having a secure salary was a frightening prospect, especially with three children to support. However, Connie encouraged Walter, and her support, along with the success of *Fast Sam*, gave him the courage he needed. And the gamble paid off. As Myers would say later on,

"Since 1977, I have never had another job other than writer."[1]

Indeed, after *Fast Sam*, Myers continued to write books at an almost nonstop pace. *It Ain't All for Nothing* (1978) was followed by *The Legend of Tarik* (1981) and *Won't Know Till I Get There* (1982), among others.

Most of Myers's works have been critical and popular successes. The *New York Times* said *Fallen Angels*, for example, was "as thought-provoking as it is entertaining."[2] *Booklist* echoed that praise: "This gut-twisting Vietnam novel . . . breaks uncharted ground."[3] Myers demonstrated how he applies his Harlem world to a range of subject matter in such books as *The Dragon Takes a Wife* (1985), a fairy tale with a contemporary twist. In the book, a dragon finds companionship with a jive-talking good fairy named Mabel Mae Jones. In *The Legend of Tarik*, a sci-fi story with a Harlem twist, the good-guy lessons are based on the spirituals Myers learned at Bible school as a child.

Myers has gained a reputation as one of the most prolific authors around. To date, he has published close to seventy books—altogether, probably more pages, he has said, than any other African American writer. One journalist called Myers the "Shaquille O'Neal of young adult literature, a playful giant who's also an unstoppable force."[4]

And yet despite his success, it still gnawed at Myers that he didn't have a college diploma. Because of this, at nearly forty, he registered at Empire State College in New York. The college gave Myers three years' credit for life experience. He earned a degree in 1984, then quickly resumed his full-time writing career.

No matter what he is writing about, Myers says, "I get close to my characters."[5] This takes a lot of work, and Myers is a very disciplined writer. He gets up early in the mornings—usually around five—and does his own method of exercise: He walks five miles (eight kilometers), wearing a twenty-pound (twelve-kilogram) vest. He returns home at about seven, showers, and then settles down to write in his office where his cat, Askia, is usually keeping his chair warm. Myers tries to write ten pages every day. Before that, he makes a story line. As he explains,

> What I'll do is outline the story first . . . I cut out pictures of all of my characters, and my wife puts them into a collage, which goes on the wall above the computer. When I walk into the room I can see the characters, and I just get very close to them. I rush through a

first draft, and then I go back and rewrite, because I can usually see what the problems are going to be ahead of me. Rewriting is more fun for me than the writing is.[6]

Myers rewrites a story as many as seven to ten times. And he never works on just one story at a time. He may be ironing out the details of one story line, rewriting another, and thinking of a third. He believes writing is not so much about talent as hard work:

> What I earnestly believe is that writing can be learned by anyone truly interested in language and literature. The trick is not to wait for inspiration, but rather to train yourself to sit down and write on a regular basis. Writers don't fail because they don't write well, they fail because they don't produce. My advice to young writers is to read as much good literature as they can so they will experience the best uses of language and the most sensitive storytelling, and then train them- selves to write on a regular basis.[7]

Aside from writing, Myers makes time for hobbies, including playing the flute and collect- ing old letters and photographs that relate to African Amercan life, which he hunts down at flea markets and auctions. Today, he has more than 100,000 historic photos in his collection. And, as usual, his life crosses over into his work. Once a rare-book dealer in London, England, told Myers about a packet of old photos that had come into his shop. They were of a real-life African princess, Sarah Forbes Bonetta, who had been rescued from slavery and brought to England where she was placed under the care of Queen Victoria. Myers found Sarah's story fascinating. Piecing together all the details of her life, he wrote the acclaimed novel, *At Her Majesty's Request: An African Princess in Victorian England* (1999).

Myers's love of history pops up in other ways as well. He likes to insert little-known historical facts into his fiction. One of the reasons he wrote the novel *The Journal of Joshua Loper: A Black Cowboy* (1999), he says, was to let readers in on the fact that 30 percent of the cowboys in the Wild West were black or Hispanic.

His interest in history was also an inspiration for his 1994 novel *Glory Field*. The book is an excellent example of Myers's talent for weaving important moments in African American history into fiction. In it, Myers traces the story of a fictional African American family from the ancestor Muhammad Bilal, who in 1753 was brought to America from Sierra Leone aboard a slave ship, to his descendants, the present-day Lewis family. *Glory Field* focuses on the family's struggle to keep its parcel of land in South Carolina and to maintain its dignity through troubled times. The book's very moving ending shows the current generation of Lewises reuniting on *Glory Field*. About the book, one reviewer said: "While some of the incidents cry out for a book of their very own, Myers has managed to sketch a valid microcosm [of black history] through this family."[8]

Myers volunteers at schools in Jersey City, New Jersey, where he and Connie live today. He also occasionally participates in reading programs in schools and libraries with basketball players from the NBA. He recently appeared with NBA legends Tiny Archibald and Willis Reed. Myers likes to talk to kids who think—as kids did in his day—that basketball is the only way out of the ghetto. He reminds them that the chances are slim that they will become star hoopers. Just as Coach Cal tells Lonnie in *Hoops*, "For every black basketball player in the NBA under six ten, there's two more out here just as good who won't see the inside of the Garden unless he's got a ticket or a broom."[9] Myers tells kids who come to hear him speak that they have a better chance of success if they attend college.

Myers is very close to his own children. His son Christopher, an artist, has illustrated some of his father's books, for example, *Monster* and a book of poetry called *Harlem* (2001). Through his children and their friends, Myers keeps up with the latest street language, which he then transfers to his books. He has to keep his ears sharp. Some readers wrote to him to say that the slang in the original edition of *The Dragon Takes a Wife* was outdated and they didn't understand it. Because of this, Myers wrote a new edition of the story using the latest slang!

Handbook for Boys

Myers's recurring themes of personal growth through error, confusing family relations, and his empathy for young people and the tough decisions they have to make are seen in three more of his books: *Handbook for Boys* (2002), *Scorpions*, and *Monster*. The volunteer work he does as a mentor inspired Myers to write *Handbook for Boys*. With this book, Myers again shows his talent at creating believable characters who sometimes goof up but who learn from their mistakes. The story is narrated by sixteen-year-old Jimmy Lynch who is in trouble with the law. When the novel opens, Jimmy is about to be sentenced to a youth facility for six months, until Duke, a sixty-year-old man who owns a barbershop, offers to take him into his "community mentoring program." The authorities also have turned another boy, Kevin, over to Duke. Jimmy and Kevin must come to Duke's shop every day to sweep the floors, clean spittoons, and do other chores they hate (they also hate each other). They call Duke's shop "the Torture Chamber" and resent his meddling in their lives. Throughout the book, Duke asks the boys an ongoing series of questions. Every answer is followed by another question. This is a system of learning known as the Socratic method. Through his questions, Duke helps the boys work through the tough choices they face on the streets. Myers subtly describes Jimmy's changing attitude. At the end, when Kevin falls back into trouble, it's his former rival, Jimmy, who goes to help him.

Myers says Duke is based on himself. He says he also wrote *Handbook* to remind the new black middle class of its responsibilities: "Now that the black middle class is growing, no one wants to be associated with the kids who aren't doing well."[10]

Scorpions and *Monster*

The idea for his Newbery Honor–winning novel *Scorpions* came to Myers one day when he was playing basketball with his sons in the park. As he tells it, "One kid we played with stopped coming to the park. I thought he had just lost his interest in the game, but then I read that he had shot someone. This bothered me quite a bit, and when something bothers me, I write about it. The issue, in my mind, was the kid having a gun. That's why I gave Jamal the gun in the book."[11]

The success of *Scorpions* illustrates Myers talent for creating complex characters and for giving seemingly depressing stories an upbeat tone. The main character, twelve-year-old Jamal Hicks, who dreams of becoming an artist, is being lured into a gang, the Scorpions. His best friend Tito tells him to stay away: "They look like thrown-away people . . . That makes me scared because I don't want to be no thrown-away guy."[12] But for Jamal, it's not that simple. There are family problems to consider: His older brother is in jail, and his family needs the bail money to get him out. His mother is having a hard time coping with everything, and his father, who drifts in and out of his life, wants Jamal to "be a man."[13] When Jamal finds himself with a gun, which one reviewer stated is a symbol of both "power and self destruction,"[14] readers see how he works through the situation to make the right decision.

Myers examines the theme of self-perception in *Monster,* his biggest commercial success to date and a book that "electrified"[15] the world of young adult books. Sixteen-year-old Steve Harmon has been charged as an accomplice to murder in the accidental shooting of a drug-store owner and is awaiting trial in an adult court. Was he the lookout in the drugstore holdup, or was he just in the wrong place at the wrong time? Steve, who was taking a filmmaking course at a school for the city's brightest kids, copes with the terror of jail and a possible life sentence by deciding to see this reality as a film script. Steve says, "Sometimes I feel like I have walked into the middle of a movie. It is a strange movie with no plot and no beginning . . . [It's] about being alone when you are not really alone and about being scared all the time. The film will be the story . . . of this experience . . . I'll call it what the lady who is the prosecutor called me. MONSTER."[16]

Myers's innovative use of the film script technique makes the story especially gripping. And Steve's growing self-doubt is contagious. Throughout the book, you don't know if Steve is guilty or not. After a while, Steve doesn't know if he is a "monster" either. About *Monster,* one reviewer said that the book is so "filled with ambiguity, [that] this fast-paced nail-biter will have you at the edge of your seat unable to put it down."[17] In *The Horn Book Magazine,* critic Patty Campbell called *Monster* a "once-in-a-decade event, a milestone comparable to [J. D. Salinger's acclaimed] *Catcher in the Rye* [1951] and S. E. Hinton's *The Outsiders* [1967]."[18]

7 Walter Dean Myers, Living Black Poet

It has been said that Walter Dean Myers's writing "redefines the images of African-Americans."[1] After he had become a successful author, an interviewer asked Myers, "Should whites write about blacks?"[2] He responded, "Of course I feel you should write about anybody you want to write about. I couldn't care less who you write about. But what very often happens is that, when you're writing about a culture that's not your own, you may hit large areas of it, but there are so many areas that you miss."[3]

Despite that statement, Myers, true to character, refuses to be pigeonholed as a "black writer." When he is referred to as such, he responds, "I know that tomorrow I might meet somebody who will tell me that 1) I am not really Black 2) I make too much of being Black 3) I am trying to deny I am Black."[4] This, he says, is an important concept for minorities to think about because "in nailing down one's racial identity one has to consider whether you identify with the people you see around you."[5] As he says, "This can be a real problem if your neighbors are crackheads. Do you identify only with the biology? White people will expect you to have rhythm and know something about the blues. Are you abandoning your race if you love Beethoven more than B. B. King?"[6]

These thoughts aren't much different from the ones Myers had when he was a ten-year-old and had become hooked on books. In many ways, he has grown, but in other ways, Myers is still the same person he was back in Harlem. Indeed, Harlem has never left him. The kid who loved hearing stories and reading about faraway places and fantasy characters has made a name writing about the place closest to him, both geographically and emotionally. Some critics of Myers's work have suggested that he is limited in range, meaning that his Harlem-based stories too often resemble each other. While they may well be variations on a similar theme, Myers says that is the point: "What I wanted to do was to portray this vital community as one that is very special to a lot of people. I wanted to show the people I knew as being as richly endowed with those universal traits of love, humor, and ambition as any in the world. That space of earth was no ghetto, it was home."[7]

Myers remained close to his foster parents, Florence and Herbert Dean, until their deaths. Herbert Dean was like a grandfather to Walter's three children and told them stories just as he had to Walter when he was young. And the Deans were proud of him, even though up until they died, they still could not understand, as Myers said, "my making a better living than they had without ever leaving the house."[8]

After he had become a parent himself, Myers would come to appreciate how much his foster parents had given him. He even learned that his foster father contributed to his writing after he once told Herbert Dean the theme of a story he had written. Mr. Dean laughed and told Myers that the story was in fact one he had told Walter as a child.

Myers's own story is less that of an angry, tormented artist than that of a complex personality who learns and grows through living and who has struggled to find a voice for his experience.

The question readers ask Myers most is how much does he take his stories from his own life? To that Myers responds, "The main character is always someone I know and part of myself. I am putting all of my life into these books."[9]

The ever busy Myers says he plans to retire "seven minutes before I die."[10]

Interview with
Walter Dean Myers

This interview was reprinted with permission by Walter Dean Myers. It was posted on http://www.harperchildrens.com.

Interviewer: You've written for many different age groups. What are the special challenges of writing for young adults? What do you like about it?

Walter Dean Myers: Being a young adult is always a traumatic age for kids. You go through the shock of being a child, directly to the responsibility of being an adult and the problems that an adult faces. You're facing the world for the first time as an individual. It's a difficult period in everybody's life. It was for me, but I keep referring back to it because it was such an exciting and trying time in my life. When you're young, you make mistakes. The big thing that's different now is that when I was a kid, you could survive your mistakes. Then, if you got into a gang fight, you hit someone with a stick or you threw a bottle . . . today kids have access to guns. The same kids that would have been in trouble and gotten a stern talking-to are now going to jail for fifteen or twenty years. Instead of having a bloody nose, you're dead. Then, you could get away with your mistakes. It's much harder living today. The values are basically the same, but it's easier to mess up.

Interviewer: A theme that runs through the books is the ever-present fear of violence. How do you hope your books will influence kids?

Walter Dean Myers: I am not interested in giving kids something that will all of a sudden change their lives. Just having kids think about it is important. I feel that kids don't think about things until after they happen. I remember one time I hitched a ride on the bumper of a cab, and I wound up being dragged a block. I was all bruised up, and afterward I thought I probably shouldn't have done that. That's typical of kids . . . You do things first, then you think about it. By the time you think about it, you're in big trouble.

Facing someone with a gun is less personal and takes less nerve than being in a fist fight—it doesn't require as much physical courage. Someone like Jamal [*Scorpions*], when faced with the idea of confronting a bully, doesn't have to draw up that physical courage, and that's really bad news.

Interviewer: In *Scorpions*, the older brother is in jail. Was the starting point of *Monster* the desire to flip the perspective and tell the story from the perspective of a jailed person?

Walter Dean Myers: I did a lot of interviews with kids in jail for *Monster*. One of the things that really shook me was that the young men did not understand how they got from the point of innocence to the ability to commit a crime. What got them there, of course, were the small moral decisions they made for which they were not punished. Many of these people in jails think of themselves as basically innocent kids who got caught up. They don't realize the process. In *Monster*, if there had been no death and if these guys had just taken the money and split, he might have felt that it was an easy thing to do, so maybe he would have gone on to do something else. When people plan their crimes, they always think that everything will work out perfectly, and it doesn't. That's what scares me. That's what I hope kids reading this book [*Monster*] will do . . . They'll think more in advance about what they're doing and the outcome.

Interviewer: What do you tell readers who want to be writers?

Walter Dean Myers: I have two skills: One skill is the ability to use language. You learn language from other people . . . from reading people who are good, so you have to be a good reader. The second skill I have is discipline. You sit down and you start something, and you have to finish it. Do you have the ability to work at this trait? You don't have a boss . . . it's not easy. Sometimes I'll add that writing is work—it's hard work, but hard doesn't mean bad.

Interviewer: What's your favorite thing a reader ever said to you?

Walter Dean Myers: I was at a school talking to very young girls, and at the end one girl came up to me and said, "You're not that much!" I was taken aback, but then I realized she had made a connection with me. She saw me as a real person. If I can give kids an idea that I'm an ordinary person who is doing something that they like a lot, that's a wonderful thing. I had the same misconceptions about authors when I was a kid. I thought you had to be at least white . . . Every author I saw when I was going to school was white, and usually dead and male. Then I met Langston Hughes, and I thought . . . he can't be an author. I initially rejected him internally, but eventually he gave me permission to be a writer. Yes, you can write about your own life, even if your life is not that glamorous.

Interviewer: How did the books you read when you were young influence you?

Walter Dean Myers: I was lucky—the English teacher in high school was just fabulous, and she turned me on to some really good literature . . . I read a lot. Reading great literature influenced me tremendously because it gave me a sense of the ideal. You reach an ideal. What's the best in life? What do you think about, hold up as wonderful? I got that through literature.

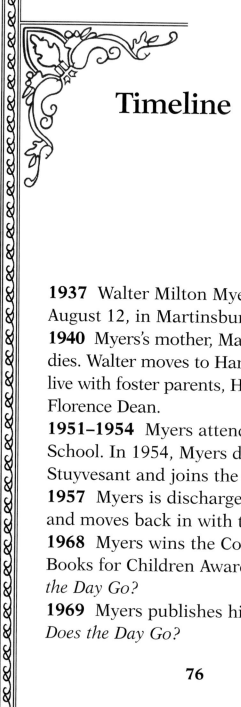

Timeline

1937 Walter Milton Myers is born on August 12, in Martinsburg, West Virginia.
1940 Myers's mother, Mary Green Myers, dies. Walter moves to Harlem, New York, to live with foster parents, Herbert and Florence Dean.
1951–1954 Myers attends Stuyvesant High School. In 1954, Myers drops out of Stuyvesant and joins the U.S. Army.
1957 Myers is discharged from the army and moves back in with the Deans.
1968 Myers wins the Council on Interracial Books for Children Award for *Where Does the Day Go?*
1969 Myers publishes his first book, *Where Does the Day Go?*

1970 Myers becomes an editor at Bobbs-Merrill, a publishing company in New York

1973 Myers marries Constance Brendel.

1975 *Fast Sam, Cool Clyde, and Stuff*, Myers's first young adult novel, is published.

1977 Myers loses his job at Bobbs-Merrill and becomes a full-time writer.

1984 Myers receives a B.A. from Empire State College.

1993 Myers publishes his first book of poems, *Brown Angels*.

2000 Myers publishes *Bad Boy,* his memoirs of growing up in Harlem. He is awarded the first ever Michael L. Printz Award for excellence in young adult literature for *Monster*.

Selected Reviews from *School Library Journal*

Crystal
July 1987

Gr 8–12—At sixteen, Crystal Brown is en route to stardom as a black fashion model. The world of money, glamour, fame, and celebrities excites and disturbs her. Her career demands increasing time away from family, friends, school, and normal adolescent concerns. As a model, Crystal confronts a temperamental photographer, sexual pressures, and a demanding agent. While Crystal's mother vicariously craves her daughter's success, her father's pride is tempered with protectiveness. In the end, Crystal is shocked into a career decision by the suicide of a once marketable model friend. In

Crystal, Myers has created a beautiful but believable teenage heroine who makes a stand for personal integrity in a competitive world. Although certain characters and situations fulfill modeling world stereotypes, Myers's knack for vivid description and dialogue shatters many illusions of stardom. Adolescents who dream of modeling and who may envy Crystal's natural gifts will find in her forthright story certain realities that are often ignored. —Gerry Larson, North Carolina

The Glory Field
November 1994

Gr 7 Up—This moving, effective novel is a sort of *Roots* for young adults. It chronicles the African American experience through the lives and times of one family, beginning in 1753 with the capture of Muhammad Bilal in Sierra Leone. He survives his journey to America on a slave ship to become the founder of a family, whose history *The Glory Field* is all about. Readers then meet one of his descendants, Lizzy, a young slave who works on a plantation in 1864 on Curry Island, South Carolina. From slavery, escape, and the Civil War, they follow the fortunes of the family to the year 1900.

Then, teenaged Elijah migrates north. Chicago of the 1930s is described through the experiences of Luvenia, sixteen; Curry Island of 1964 is seen through the eyes of Tommy, also sixteen. The last part of the story is set in the present and focuses on Malcolm and Shep, teenaged cousins who have come to Curry from New York City for a family reunion. The decades pass swiftly and are connected by characters who appear in one segment of the saga and reappear later as survivors from the past or as memories. Each part of the story ends on a hopeful note, yet each is unfinished. Readers are left to wonder what happened to various people; sometimes an answer is provided, but more often not. The vast array of characters plays out their lives challenged and beset by problems of racism, poverty, and identity. The anchors in their lives are family and their love for one another and their land. A beautifully written, powerful book. —Carol Jones Collins, New Jersey

Mop, Moondance, and the Nagasaki Knights
September 1992

Gr 4–6—The characters from *Me, Mop, and the Moondance Kid* (Delacorte, 1988) return in another novel of baseball and friendship. Again, the best part of the book is the first-person narration of T. J., a cheerful, funny, and appealing protagonist. Myers beautifully captures the boy's sometimes confused view of the world. Yet through all of his troubles, T. J. maintains his positive attitude. The novel is set against the backdrop of an international baseball tournament featuring T. J.'s team, along with teams from Japan, Mexico, and France. The French players are definitely the coolest. Although they know little about baseball, they carry everything off with a certain humorous savoir faire [know-how]. More serious is T. J.'s discovery that a teammate is homeless. It's refreshing in a novel dealing with sports to find a main character who is a mediocre player. And, in general, the level of play described is closer to what actually happens at a Little League game than in some other books. In all, it's nice to see this cast again. —Todd Morning, Illinois

A Place Called Heartbreak: A Story of Vietnam **Illustrated by Frederick Porter** **June 1993**

Gr 5–9—In a book that reads more like a novel than nonfiction, Myers tells the story of Col. [Colonel] Fred V. Cherry, U.S.A.F. (Ret.), who was a prisoner of the North Vietnamese from October 22, 1965 to February 12, 1973. He relates how Cherry, an African American, overcame obstacles during his youth to attend college and fulfill his boyhood dream of becoming an Air Force fighter pilot. It was on a mission from Thailand to North Vietnam that squadron leader Cherry was shot down, thus becoming the first black pilot to become a prisoner of war in North Vietnam. His experiences there, as well as some background information and his present feelings about the Vietnam War, are presented in well-organized hi/lo prose; this is accomplished without over-simplification or generalizations. Myers indicates in the notes that he had extensive interviews with his subject; it is likely that these were the source of the dialogue and his internal thoughts. In any event, they ring true and contribute greatly to holding readers' interest. Several well-rendered full-page line illustrations augment and illuminate the text. Unfortunately, there is no index. —David A. Lindsey, Washington

Scorpions
1988

Jamal, who is pressured to become the leader of the Scorpions gang, worries about school, family, and the rough kids on the street. When a fellow gang member gives him a gun, Jamal suddenly gains a new level of respect from his enemies. A realistic look at a boy who wants to do the right thing but gets caught up in the culture of violence. A Newbery Honor selection.

Somewhere in the Darkness
May 1992

Gr 7–10—A poignant story of motherless, fourteen-year-old Jimmy Little, whose convict father takes him on a search for truth, identity, and family. Whisked away from the stability of a home life with his devoted grandmother, Mama Jean, Jimmy confronts the harsh realities of his father's life on the run. Jailed for his involvement in an armed robbery and falsely accused of killing a man, Crab escapes from prison to convince his son of his innocence. What Jimmy discovers is a man desperate to establish a relationship with his son but unable to break free of a lifestyle of stealing and moving on that leaves little room for security. On their highway odyssey, Crab becomes increasingly sick with a kidney ailment. Following a climactic encounter with the man who accused him, Crab is again arrested and hospitalized. For Jimmy, the flicker of hope that he and his father might work things out becomes a realization that love is built on trust, concern, and honesty. Through terse dialogue and characterization, Myers conveys a powerful message about the need for parent and child to believe in and respect one another. By the story's end, the boy understands that to fully appreciate someone else's life you must first give meaning to your own. Whether from urban or rural backgrounds, single or double parent families, readers will find this universal journey of self-discovery gratifying. —Gerry Larson, North Carolina

Shadow of the Red Moon
Illustrated by Christopher Myers
1995

Gr 5–9—The Okalians have survived a meteor collision and a long exile from their homeland, and now face certain annihilation at the hands of the Fens, a group of marauding children. Jon, a fifteen-year-old Okalian, is sent by his parents into the Wilderness to return to the Ancient Land and restore their race to its former greatness. On his journey he teams up with a young girl, her brother, and a black unicorn. Using spare prose and lean characters, Myers masterfully creates a world in which adults are nearly nonexistent and children struggle to establish a life for

themselves. They face endless dangers in their environment, including the temptation to escape reality. Forced to redefine a world gone wrong, they return to ancient traditions and values, and ultimately learn to see beyond human differences. YAs [young adults] will enjoy the fantasy and adventure, while mature readers will recognize the story's vivid parallels with modern society. While this tale is narrated in gray and somber tones, in the end the meteor dust is settling, and the red moon offers a beam of hope.
—Tim Rausch, Utah

List of
Selected Works

At Her Majesty's Request: An African Princess in Victorian England. New York: Scholastic, 1999.

Brown Angels: An Album of Pictures and Verse. New York: HarperCollins, 1993.

Crystal. New York: Viking, 1987.

Darnell Rock Reporting. New York: Delacorte Press, 1994.

The Dragon Takes a Wife. Illustrated by Ann Grifalconi. Indianapolis, IN: Bobbs-Merrill, 1972.

Fallen Angels. New York: Scholastic, 1988.

Fast Sam, Cool Clyde, and Stuff. New York: Viking, 1975.

Fly, Jimmy, Fly! Illustrated by Moneta Barnett. New York: Putnam, 1974.

Glorious Angels: An Album of Pictures and Verse. New York: HarperCollins, 1995.

The Glory Field. New York: Scholastic, 1994.

Harlem: A Poem. Illustrated by Christopher Myers. New York: Scholastic, 1997.

Hoops. New York: Delacorte Press, 1981.

How Mr. Monkey Saw the Whole World. New York: Doubleday, 1996.

It Ain't All for Nothin'. New York: Viking, 1978.

The Legend of Tarik. New York: Viking, 1981.

Malcolm X: By Any Means Necessary. New York: Scholastic, 1993.

Me, Mop, and the Moondance Kid. New York: Delacorte Press, 1988.

Mojo and the Russians. New York: Viking, 1977.

Monster. Illustrated by Christopher Myers. New York: HarperCollins, 1999

Motown and Didi: A Love Story. New York: Viking, 1987.

The Mouse Rap. New York: HarperCollins, 1990.

Mr. Monkey and the Gotcha Bird. Illustrated by Leslie Morrill. New York: Delacorte, 1984.

The Nicholas Factor. New York: Viking, 1983.

Now Is Your Time! The African-American Struggle for Freedom. New York: HarperCollins, 1991.

145th Street: Short Stories. New York: Delacorte Press, 2000.

One More River to Cross: An African American Photograph Album. New York: Harcourt Brace, 1996.

The Outside Shot. New York: Delacorte, 1984.

The Righteous Revenge of Artemis Bonner. New York: HarperCollins, 1992.

Scorpions. New York: Harper & Row, 1988.

Slam! New York: Scholastic, 1996.

Somewhere in the Darkness. New York: Scholastic, 1992.

Where Does the Day Go? Illustrated by Leo Carty. New York: Parents Magazine Press, 1969.

Won't Know Till I Get There. New York: Viking Press, 1982.

The Young Landlords. New York: Viking, 1979.

List of Selected Awards

Margaret A. Edwards Award, in honor of an author's lifetime achievement for writing books that have been popular with teenagers (1994)

Fallen Angels (1988)
American Library Association Best Books for Young Adults (1988)
American Library Association Quick Picks for Reluctant Young Adult Readers (1988)
Coretta Scott King Author Award for Fiction (1988)
Parents' Choice Award (1988)
School Library Journal Best Book of the Year (1988)

Fast Sam, Cool Clyde, and Stuff (1975)
American Library Association Notable Books (1975)

Harlem: A Poem (1997)

American Library Association Best Book for
  Young Adults (1998)
American Library Association Notable Children's
  Book (1998)
Caldecott Honor Book (1998)
Coretta Scott King Honor Book (1998)

Hoops (1982)

American Library Association Best Books for
  Young Adults Citation (1982)
Edgar Allan Poe Award runner-up (1982)

Malcolm X: By Any Means Necessary (1994)

American Library Association Best Books for
  Young Adults (1994)
Coretta Scott King Award for Nonfiction (1994)
International Reading Association Teachers'
  Choice (1994)
The Library of Congress Children's Book of the
  Year (1994)

Monster (1999)

American Library Association Best Book for
  Young Adults (1999)
Boston Globe/Horn Book Honor Book (1999)
Coretta Scott King Author Honor Book (1999)
Michael L. Printz Award (2000)

National Book Award Finalist (1999)

Motown and Didi: A Love Story **(1984)**
Coretta Scott King Award for Fiction (1985)

***Now Is Your Time!: The African-American
Struggle for Freedom*** **(1991)**
American Library Association Best Books for
Young Adults and Notable Books for
Children (1992)
Coretta Scott King Award for Nonfiction (1992)
National Council of Teachers of English
Orbis Pictus Award for Outstanding
Nonfiction (1992)

Scorpions **(1988)**
American Library Association Best Book for
Young Adults (1988)
American Library Association Notable
Children's Book (1988)
Newbery Honor Book (1989)

Somewhere in the Darkness **(1992)**
American Library Association Best Books for
Young Adults, Notable Books for Children
(1993)
Boston Globe/Horn Book Honor Book (1992)
Booklist Editors Choice (1992)

Coretta Scott King Author Honor Book (1993)
Newbery Honor Book (1993)

***Where Does the Day Go?* (1969)**
Council on Interracial Books for Children
 Award (1969)

***Won't Know Till I Get There* (1982)**
Parents' Choice Award (1982)

***The Young Landlords* (1979)**
American Library Association Notable Book
 Citation and American Library Association
 Best Books for Young Adults Citation (1979)
Coretta Scott King Award for Fiction (1980)

Glossary

ally To support or follow.

black English A dialect of English with its own working grammar, spoken primarily by some African Americans.

devour To soak up or digest in immense quantities.

existentialism A literary and philosophical movement that is based on the belief that each person exists as an individual in a purposeless universe.

hyperactive Excessively active.

hoop A slang verb, meaning to play basketball.

mentor A leader or a guide who voluntarily gives instruction or advice.

Michael L. Printz Award A young adult literature award established in 2000 to recognize excellence in the field of young adult books. The award is given by the Young Adult Library Services Association, which is a division of the American Library Association. The award is named for Michael L. Printz, a former school librarian in Kansas, and is given to one book per year and up to four runners-up. Walter Dean Myers was awarded the first Printz for *Monster* in 2000.

pigeonhole To classify something systematically.

premise A supposition; the idea behind something.

rap A form of street language; a language spoken in verse.

rejection slips Letters from editors of books or magazines saying they aren't interested in publishing the material an author has sent them.

speech impediment A speaking disorder, such as stuttering.

spittoon A jarlike container to spit in.

stiletto A small knife with a sharp thin blade.

vice A bad or harmful habit.

voluntary segregation Intentional separation, that is, not one imposed by law. In this case, black colleges would not be segregated by law but for cultural reasons.

For More Information

Web Sites

Due to the changing nature of Internet links, the Rosen Publishing Group, Inc., has developed an online list of Web sites related to the subject of this book. This site is updated regularly. Please use this link to access the list:

http://www.rosenlinks.com/lab/wdmy

For Further Reading

Camus, Albert. *The Stranger.* New York: Vintage Books, 1989.

Ostrom, Hans. *A Langston Hughes Encyclopedia.* Westport, CT: Greenwood Press, 2001.

Rush, T., et al., eds. *Black American Writers: Past and Present.* Metuchen, NJ: Scarecrow Press, 1975, pp. 563–564.

Salinger, J. D. *The Catcher in the Rye.* New York: Little Brown, 1951.

Senick, G., ed. *Children's Literature Review.* Vol. 16, Winter 1989. Detroit, MI: Gale Group, pp. 134–144.

Bibliography

Biographical information on Walter Dean Myers. Retrieved 2002 (http://www.falcon.jmu.edu/~ranseyil/myers.htm).

Biographical information on Walter Dean Myers. Retrieved 2002 (http://www.carr.lib.md.ud/mae/myer/myers.htm).

Discussion of Walter Dean Myers's *Somewhere in the Darkness*. Retrieved 2002 (http://www.umcs.maine.edu/~orono/collabortive/somehwhere.html).

Davis, T., and T. Harris, eds. *Dictionary of Literary Biography: Afro-American Fiction Writers after 1955*. Vol. 33. Detroit, MI: Gale Group, 1984, pp. 199–202.

Fischer, Marilyn. "Learning About Walter Dean Myers." Compiled by Marilyn Fischer, Carol Levandowski, and Carol Marlowe. Retrieved 2002 (www.scils.rutgers.edu/special/kay/smith.html).

Hedblad, Alan, ed. *Something About the Author*, Vol. 111. Detroit, MI: Gale Group, 2000, pp. 203–225.

Myers, Walter Dean. *Bad Boy*. New York: HarperCollins, 2001.

Myers, Waler Dean. *Fallen Angels*. New York: Scholastic, 1988.

Myers, Walter Dean. *Fast Sam, Cool Clyde, and Stuff*. New York: Viking, 1975.

Myers, Walter Dean. *Hoops*. New York: Delacorte Press, 1981.

Myers, Walter Dean. Margaret A. Edwards Award Acceptance Speech. Reprinted in *Journal of Youth Services in Libraries*, Vol. 8, No. 2, Winter 1995, pp. 129–133.

Myers, Walter Dean. *Monster*. New York: HarperCollins, 1999.

Myers, Walter Dean. *Motown and Didi: A Love Story*. New York: Viking, 1984.

Myers, Walter Dean. *Scorpions*. New York: Harper & Row, 1988.

Myers, Walter Dean. *Somewhere in the Darkness*. New York: Scholastic, 1992

Needham, Nancy R. "Making Intellect Cool." *NEA Today*, December 1991, p. 9.

Patrick-Wexler, Diane. *Walter Dean Myers*. Austin, TX: Steck-Vaughn Company, 1996.

Smith, Amanda "Walter Dean Myers: This Award-Winning Author for Young People Tells It Like It Is." *Publishers Weekly*, July 20, 1992, pp. 217–218.

Sutton, Roger. "Threads in Our Cultural Fabric." *School Library Journal*, Vol. 40, No. 6, (June 1994), pp. 24–28.

"Teenreads Talks to Walter Dean Myers." Teenreads.com. February 4, 2001. Retrieved 2002 (http://www.teanreads.com).

Telgen, D., ed. *Something About the Author*. Vol. 71. Detroit, MI: Gale Group, 1993, pp. 133–137.

"Walter Dean Myers in His Own Words": Autobiographical sketch of Walter Dean Myers for African American literature book club. 2002, AALBC.com. Retrieved September 2002 (www.aalbc.com/authors/walter1.htm).

West, Mark I. "Harlem Connections: Teaching
   Walter Dean Myers's *Scorpions*
   in Conjunction with Paul Laurence
   Dunbar's *The Sport of the Gods.*" *ALAN
   Review*, Vol. 26, No. 2, Winter 1999.

Source Notes

Introduction
1. Interview with Walter Dean Myers,
   Teenreads.com, February 4, 2000. Retrieved
   September 2002 (http://www.teenreads.com/
   authors/au-myers-walterdean.asp).
2. Telgen, D., ed., *Something About the Author*,
   Vol. 71 (Detroit, MI: Gale Group, 1993),
   pp. 133–137.
3. Walter Dean Myers, *The Mouse Rap* (New
   York: Harper & Row, 1990), p. 3.
4. Walter Dean Myers, *Hoops* (New York:
   Delacorte, Press, 1981), p. 17.
5. Ibid., p. 43

Chapter 1
1. Sarah Brennan, Review of *Bad Boy*,
   Teenreads.com. Retrieved September 2002
   (http://www.teenreads.com/reviews/
   0060295236).

2. Autobiographical sketch written for the *Fifth Book of Junior Authors and Illustrators* (New York: H. W. Wilson, 1983). Retrieved August 2002 (http://www.edupaperback.org/authorbios/Myers_WalterDean.html).

3. Walter Dean Myers, *Bad Boy* (New York: HarperCollins, 2001), p. 9.

4. Author profile of Walter Dean Myers, Teenreads.com. Retrieved August 2002 (http://www.teenreads.com/authors/au-myers-walterdean.asp).

5. Walter Dean Myers, *Bad Boy* (New York: HarperCollins, 2001), p. 7.

6. Autobiographical sketch written for the *Fifth Book of Junior Authors and Illustrators* (New York: H. W. Wilson, 1983). Retrieved August 2002 (http://www.edupaperback.org/authorbios/Myers_WalterDean.html).

7. Walter Dean Myers, *The Mouse Rap* (New York: Harper & Row, 1990), p. 8.

8. Walter Dean Myers, *Bad Boy* (New York: HarperCollins, 2001), p. 14.

Chapter 2

1. Jim Higgins, "Former 'Bad Boy' Taps into Youths' Minds, Struggles," *Milwaukee Journal Sentinel*, May 26, 2002. Retrieved August 2002 (http://www.jsonline.com).

2. Walter Dean Myers, *Bad Boy* (New York: HarperCollins, 2001), p. 18.

3. Ibid., p. 23.
4. Ibid., p. 45.
5. Ibid., p. 45.
6. Author profile of Walter Dean Myers, Teenreads.com. Retrieved August 2002 (http://www.teenreads.com/authors/ au-myers-walterdean.asp).
7. Walter Dean Myers, *Hoops* (New York: Delacorte Press, 1981), p. 32.
8. Walter Dean Myers, *Bad Boy* (New York: HarperCollins, 2001), p. 92.
9. Ibid., p. 92.
10. Interview with Walter Dean Myers, Teenreads.com, June 5, 2001. Retrieved August 2002 (http://www.teenreads.com/author/ au-myers-walterdean.asp).
11. Walter Dean Myers quoted in a discussion of *Somewhere in the Darkness*. Retrieved August 2002 (http://www.umcs.maine.edu/~orono/ collaborative/somewhere.html).

Chapter 3
1. Jim Higgins, "Former 'Bad Boy' Taps into Youths' Minds, Struggles," *Milwaukee Journal. Sentinel*, May 26, 2002. Retrieved August 2002 (http://www.jsonline.com).
2. Walter Dean Myers, *Somewhere in the Darkness* (New York: Scholastic, 1993), p. 3.
3. Walter Dean Myers, *Bad Boy* (New York: HarperCollins, 2001), p. 111.

4. Walter Dean Myers, *Slam!* (New York: Scholastic, 1996), p. 63.

5. Ibid., p. 119.

6. Author profile of Walter Dean Myers, Teenreads.com. Retrieved August 2002 (http://www.teenreads.com/author/ au-myers-walterdean.asp).

7. Walter Dean Myers, *Bad Boy* (New York: HarperCollins, 2001), p. 126.

8. *Walter Dean Myers in His Own Words*, African American Literature Book Club. Retrieved September 2002 (http://www.aalbc.com/ authors/walter1.htm).

9. Walter Dean Myers, *Bad Boy* (New York: HarperCollins, 2001), p. 105.

10. Sarah Brennan, Review of *Bad Boy*, Teenreads.com. Retrieved September 2002 (http://www.teenreads.com/reviews/0060295236).

11. Walter Dean Myers, *Bad Boy* (New York: HarperCollins, 2001), p. 97.

12. Jim Higgins, "Former 'Bad Boy' Taps into Youths' Minds, Struggles," *Milwaukee Journal Sentinel*, May 26, 2002. Retrieved August 2002 (http://www.jsonline.com).

13. Walter Dean Myers, *Bad Boy* (New York: HarperCollins, 2001), p. 139.

14. Ibid., p. 128.

15. Ibid., p. 177.

Chapter 4

1. Walter Dean Myers, *Bad Boy* (New York: HarperCollins, 2001), p. 153.
2. Walter Dean Myers, *Fallen Angels* (New York: Scholastic, 1988), p. 35.
3. Albert Camus, *The Stranger*, translated by Matthew Ward (New York: Vintage Books, 1989), p. 3.
4. Walter Dean Myers, *Bad Boy* (New York: HarperCollins, 2001), p. 172.
5. Ibid., p. 201.
6. Walter Dean Myers, *Fallen Angels* (New York: Scholastic, 1988), p. 119.
7. Ibid., pp. 14–15
8. Walter Dean Myers, *Bad Boy* (New York: HarperCollins, 2001), p. 200.

Chapter 5

1. Reader review of *Fast Sam, Cool Clyde, and Stuff*, Amazon.com. Retrieved August 2002 (http://www.amazon.com).

Chapter 6

1. Jim Higgins, "Former 'Bad Boy' Taps into Youths' Minds, Struggles," *Milwaukee Journal Sentinel*, May 26, 2002. Retrieved August 2002 (http://www.jsonline.com).
2. Review of *Fallen Angels*, *New York Times Book Review*. Date not available.

3. Review of *Fallen Angels*, *Booklist*. Date not available.

4. Jim Higgins, "Former 'Bad Boy' Taps into Youths' Minds, Struggles," *Milwaukee Journal Sentinel*, May 26, 2002. Retrieved August 2002 (http://www.jsonline.com).

5. Author profile of Walter Dean Myers, Teenreads.com. Retrieved August 2002 (http://www.teenreads.com/author/ au-myers-walterdean.asp).

6. Ibid.

7. Interview with Walter Dean Myers, Teenreads.com, February 4, 2000. Retrieved August 2002 (http://www.teenreads.com/author/ au-myers-walterdean.asp).

8. Kathleen Karr, Review of *Glory Field*, *Scholastic Books*.

9. Walter Dean Myers, *Hoops* (New York: Delacorte Press, 1981), p. 70.

10. Jim Higgins, "Former 'Bad Boy' Taps into Youths' Minds, Struggles," *Milwaukee Journal Sentinel*, May 26, 2002. Retrieved August 2002 (http://www.jsonline.com).

11. Interview with Walter Dean Myers, *Booklist*. Date not available.

12. Walter Dean Myers, *Scorpions* (New York: Harper & Row, 1988), p. 161.

13. Ibid., p. 94.

14. Mark I. West, "Harlem Connections: Teaching

Walter Dean Myers's *Scorpions* in Conjunction with Paul Laurence Dunbar's *The Sport of the Gods*," *The ALAN Review*, Vol. 26, No. 2, Winter 1999.

15. Jim Higgins, "Former 'Bad Boy' Taps into Youths' Minds, Struggles," *Milwaukee Journal Sentinel*, May 26, 2002. Retrieved August 2002 (http://www.jsonline.com).

16. Walter Dean Myers, *Monster*, illustrated by Christopher Myers (New York: HarperCollins, 1999), pp. 3–5.

17. Tammy L. Currier, Review of *Monster*, Teenreads.com, 2001. Retrieved August 2002 (http://www.teenreads.com/reviews/0060295236).

18. Patty Cambell, Review of *Monster*, *The Horn Book Magazine*, November/December 1999, pp. 769–773.

Chapter 7

1. Telgen, D., ed., *Something About the Author*, Vol. 71 (Detroit, MI: Gale Group, 1993), pp. 133–137.

2. Roger Sutton, "Threads in Our Cultural Fabric," *School Library Journal*, Vol. 40, No. 6, June 1994, p. 26.

3. Ibid.

4. Interview with Walter Dean Myers, Teenreads.com, June 5, 2001. Retrieved August 2002 (http://www.teenreads.com/authors/au-myers-walterdean.asp).

5. Ibid.

6. Ibid.

7. Autobiographical sketch written for the *Fifth Book of Junior Authors and Illustrators* (New York: H. W. Wilson, 1983). Retrieved August 2002 (http://www.edupaperback.org/authorbios/Myers_WalterDean.html).

8. Ibid.

9. Jim Higgins, "Former 'Bad Boy' Taps into Youths' Minds, Struggles," *Milwaukee Journal Sentinel*, May 26, 2002. Retrieved August 2002 (http://www.jsonline.com).

10. Interview with Walter Dean Myers, *Booklist*, 2001.

Index

About the Author

Karen Burshtein is a writer, author, translator, and photo editor.

Photo Credits

Cover and p. 2 © Constance Myers;

Designer: Tahara Hasan; Editor: Annie Sommers